Genre Biography

Essential Question
How do people from different cultures contribute to a community?

Judy Baca

by Anna Harris

Chapter 1
Young Judy Baca 2

Chapter 2
The Great Wall of Los Angeles 8

Chapter 3
More Recent Work 12

Respond to Reading 15

PAIRED READ Vibrant Los Angeles 16

Glossary/Index 19

Focus on Social Studies 20

CHAPTER 1

Young Judy Baca

Do you think "real" art hangs only in dusty frames on the walls of art museums? Think again! Some people create large artworks on blank walls. These artworks are called **murals**.

Judy Baca is an American mural artist. She has painted or helped organize the painting of over 2,000 murals. Judy was born in 1946. Her family is originally from Mexico. As a young girl, Judy lived in Los Angeles with her mother, two aunts, and a grandmother she adored. Her mother worked in a tire factory. Her grandmother cared for her while her mother earned money to feed the family.

This mural, which features an elephant and a peace dove, brightens up a parking building.

California

Los Angeles

UNITED STATES

N

MEXICO

When Judy was six, her life changed. Her mother married and the pair moved to another part of Los Angeles. The rest of Judy's family stayed behind in the old neighborhood. Judy had always spoken in Spanish, but in the new neighborhood, she wasn't allowed to speak Spanish at school. She had few Mexican American classmates.

At first, Judy struggled to pronounce and understand English words. Often, the teacher gave Judy art supplies so that she could draw or paint when she couldn't follow lessons. She soon grew to love painting. When she finished school, she became the first person in her family to go to college. She studied modern art.

After college, Judy taught art at her old high school. Then, in 1970, she got a job working for the city council of Los Angeles. She taught art in the parks of a neighborhood called Boyle Heights. Different groups of teenagers hung out in these parks, and they did not get along. Judy asked 20 of the teens to help her paint a mural. Sometimes the teens' graffiti divided the neighborhood. Judy wanted them to learn to work together without fighting. She hoped the mural would be a good way to help them realize that the neighborhood belonged to all of them.

Some people in the community tried to disrupt work on the mural, but Judy wouldn't quit. She made the project work. When the mural was finished, people loved it, and members of the public often placed flowers and candles underneath it. Boyle Heights was a Mexican American neighborhood. The mural appealed to people's Mexican **heritage**. It became a symbol of **unity**. The mural was called *Mi Abuelita (My Grandmother)*. It showed a Mexican American grandmother with outstretched arms. She looked as if she was offering a hug.

Mi Abuelita, which means "My Grandmother," was painted in a park in Boyle Heights.

The success of *Mi Abuelita* helped Judy start a citywide mural program. She designed the murals and hired young people to organize the crews that would paint them. From 1974, these young people created about 500 murals in the streets of Los Angeles.

Sometimes, city officials didn't like Judy's ideas for murals. Judy wanted the program to have as much freedom as possible. So in 1976, she helped start another group called the Social and Public Art Resource Center, or SPARC. SPARC's goal is to create art for people of all different backgrounds and cultures.

Artist Rip Cronk painted this mural for SPARC in 1989.

Wendy Connett/Alamy

The Murals of Mexico

Murals have a long history in Mexico. The ancient Maya painted images on the walls of their temples. Much later, in the 1900s, there were *Los Tres Grandes*—three great Mexican mural artists. Their names were Diego Rivera, José Clemente Orozco, and David Alfaro Siqueiros. These men painted murals to comment on social conditions in Mexico. Judy Baca admired their work.

David Alfaro Siqueiros painted this image of women and their babies.

CHAPTER 2

The Great Wall of Los Angeles

In 1976, Judy and SPARC were asked to paint a mural along a lengthy concrete wall in Los Angeles. Los Angeles is made up of people from many different cultures. Judy wanted to show that these people all contributed to the area. She decided to show their struggles and the things they achieved.

Judy talked to history experts and local people before creating a design for the mural. There aren't only famous men and women on the mural. It also tells the stories of everyday people. It shows the history of California.

The mural is called *The Great Wall of Los Angeles*, and it starts in 20,000 B.C. One section shows the Native American people who lived in the area. Another section shows the arrival of Spanish explorers. The mural also shows a period of Mexican control and the **immigrants** that later came to California. It shows the poor treatment some received. It shows black and Hispanic people fighting for equal rights.

This section of *The Great Wall* shows the Native American people who first lived in the area.

This section of *The Great Wall* shows Asian Americans gaining U.S. citizenship.

The Great Wall of Los Angeles is 13 feet high and half a mile long, making it one of the longest murals on the planet. Over 400 people helped to paint it from 1976 to 1983. Many of these people were teenagers who came from all different backgrounds. So far, it has taken about 75,000 hours to paint *The Great Wall*. However, Judy isn't done yet. Right now, she is organizing designs that will show the latest issues and events!

This team of painters worked on *The Great Wall of Los Angeles* in the 1980s.

"I hope that when people see this mural they forget all their prejudices and try to live with all people, no matter what race, in peace."

—16-year-old *Great Wall* painter Sergio Moreno

Looking after *The Great Wall*

The Great Wall is getting old—some parts have been around for more than 40 years. The mural has coped with sun, rain, and pollution. The colors were fading and some paint was peeling off. Now, the mural is getting a facelift. A team of people is slowly cleaning and repainting it. A new group of teens is working side-by-side with some of the original *Great Wall* painters. Together, they're bringing all the bright colors and images back!

Judy is helping a team of people to clean and repaint *The Great Wall*.

CHAPTER 3

More Recent Work

In 1996, Judy started the Digital Mural Lab, where people use computers to create murals. The first lab project was called *Witnesses to L.A. History*. Judy and college students made six large **digital images**. Each image stood for a different cultural group. Judy wanted to show that all of these groups are important. They all helped the city to grow and thrive. They are all part of the **multiethnic** history of Los Angeles. These murals were hung in California Plaza.

This mural shows Biddy Mason, who was freed from slavery after arriving in California. Later, Biddy fed and housed the poor and helped start the first elementary school for black children in the area.

"Witnesses to the History of Los Angeles: Biddy Mason" A student-produced public art project by the UCLA SPARC César Chávez Digital/Mural Lab conducted by Professor Judith F. Baca ©1996.

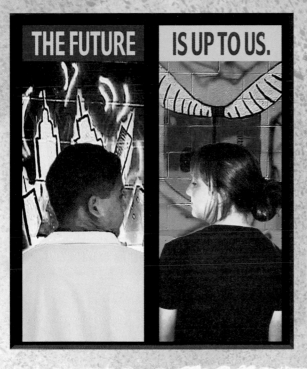

THE FUTURE IS UP TO US.

This banner, from the Shoulder to Shoulder Project, shows two teens "talking" about the future.

Human Relations Commission Shoulder to Shoulder Program. Courtesy of SPARC (www.sparcmurals.org)

The lab has been used for other projects, too. In 1999, 125 14-year-olds came together for the Shoulder to Shoulder Project. They were from different backgrounds and different cultures. Each teen was teamed up with another they would not usually meet. The teens talked about racism and stereotypes. Then they created artworks that showed what they had learned. They included some of the things they said in the artworks, too. The art was made into banners. Hundreds of these banners were hung all over Los Angeles.

Los Angeles is known as the city of murals. This is partly because of Judy. Judy Baca made Los Angeles a more colorful place. Her murals show events and ideas that are important to the people from the neighborhoods in which the murals were painted. Judy helped fill the streets of Los Angeles with images. These images show the struggles, hopes, and dreams of the city's people.

442 ND JAPANESE AMERICANS

JEWISH AMERICAN

CALIFORNIA AQUEDUCT

The Great Wall of Los Angeles could be Judy Baca's greatest achievement.

"Have the biggest vision you can! If you can't dream it, it cannot occur."

—Judy Baca

Respond to Reading

Summarize

Use details from *Judy Baca* to summarize the selection. Your graphic organizer may help you.

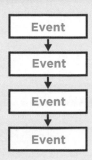

Text Evidence

1. How do you know that *Judy Baca* is a nonfiction text? What kind of nonfiction is it? How do you know? GENRE

2. What are four words or phrases on pages 3 and 4 that show events in order? SEQUENCE

3. What do you think the word *citywide* on page 6 means? COMPOUND WORDS

4. Write about five of Baca's projects, in the order in which they occurred. WRITE ABOUT READING

Compare Texts

Read about three interesting neighborhoods in Judy Baca's hometown of Los Angeles.

Vibrant Los Angeles

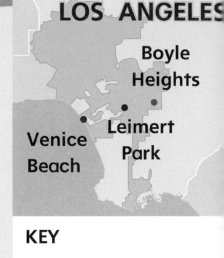

LOS ANGELES

Boyle Heights

Venice Beach

Leimert Park

KEY

▪ City of Los Angeles

Do you want to check out some fun communities in Los Angeles?

Leimert Park

Leimert Park is in south Los Angeles. It is home to many artists and musicians. Famous singers Ray Charles and Ella Fitzgerald once lived in Leimert Park. Today, Leimert Park has clubs where people can go to hear jazz music. It also has the longest-running hip-hop open-mic in the world. Anyone from the audience can perform. Another organization, The World Stage, supports local music and literature.

Boyle Heights

Boyle Heights is in east Los Angeles. It has a large Hispanic population. One popular street corner in Boyle Heights is Mariachi Plaza. The members of numerous mariachi bands, dressed in charro suits, have gathered at Mariachi Plaza since the 1930s. They play music together in the evenings. People drive up and listen to the music. They hire their favorite bands to perform at restaurants, weddings, and parties.

Mariachi musicians perform at Mariachi Plaza.

Venice Beach

Venice Beach is in west Los Angeles. A wide path runs along the beach. Many street performers gather along this path, which gives the area a circus-like feel. Venice Beach also attracts people who aren't scared to take a tumble. It

Ball players test their skills at Venice Beach.

has an area for rope climbers and acrobats. Basketball players can be seen practicing their skills on the ball courts, too. A number of NBA stars played on these courts. They hung out at Venice Beach before they were famous.

Bill Bachmann/Photo Researchers/Getty Images

Make Connections

What skills or talents do people bring to each of the three neighborhoods? ESSENTIAL QUESTION

In what ways is Judy Baca similar to the people from the three neighborhoods? In what ways is she different? TEXT TO TEXT

Glossary

digital images *(DI-juh-tuhl I-mij-iz)* images made using a computer *(page 12)*

heritage *(HER-uh-tij)* ideas and traditions handed down from the past *(page 4)*

immigrants *(I-muh-gruhnts)* people who move to the U.S. from other countries *(page 8)*

multiethnic *(MUHL-tee-ETH-nik)* made up of people from many different cultures *(page 12)*

murals *(MYEW-ruhlz)* large artworks painted on walls *(page 2)*

unity *(YEW-nuh-tee)* a feeling of togetherness or agreement *(page 4)*

Index

Boyle Heights, *4, 5, 17*

digital images, *12*

The Great Wall of Los Angeles, 8–11, 14

Leimert Park, *16*

Los Tres Grandes, 7

Mexican Americans, *3, 4*

Mi Abuelita, 4–6

murals, *2, 4, 6–8, 10–12, 14*

Venice Beach, *18*

Focus on Social Studies

Purpose To design a mural for your neighborhood

What to Do

 Step 1 With a partner, choose a blank wall in your neighborhood.

Step 2 Find out more about the area around the wall. You can focus on the past or the present. It is okay to use people or events that are not well known.

Step 3 Choose one event, person, or group from the area. With your partner, list the most important things you learned.

Step 4 Design a mural about your subject. Map out the main images on a piece of paper or a computer. You could also find out who owns the wall and show them your design. If you are lucky, they might ask you to paint the mural on the wall!

Conclusion What did you learn about your neighborhood?